The Secret of Achieving Dominion

Tom Tirivangani

THE SECRET OF
ACHIEVING DOMINION

Published by
Tom Tirivangani Press and Publications
200 Sanford Ave North, Hamilton, Ontario
Canada L8L5Z8

Copyright © 2024 by Tom Tirivangani
All rights reserved. All rights reserved.
No part of this publication may be reproduced, stored in a retrieval system, or transmitted in any form or by any means except in the case of a brief quotation printed in articles or reviews without prior permission in writing from the publisher

First Printing, 2024

Unless otherwise identified, Scripture quotations are taken from the New King James Version®. Copyright © 1982 by Thomas Nelson. Used by permission. All rights reserved.

Scripture quotations identified NIV are taken from the NEW INTERNATIONAL VERSION, Holy Bible, New International Version®, NIV® Copyright ©1973, 1978, 1984, 2011 by Biblica, Inc.® Used by permission. All rights reserved worldwide.

Contents

1 Opening the windows of life 1
2 Reflections 5
3 Milestones are windows of opportunity 17
4 Don't Underestimate the Power of Planning 31
5 God First: Prioritizing Your Relationship with Him 39
6 Dominion Through Prayer and Fasting 45
7 Achieving Dominion by Restoring Family Harmony 55
8 Obtaining Dominion through Financial Stewardship 61
9 Dominion through Embracing Your Divine Assignment 65

1

Opening the windows of life

"It pays to begin well." -Prophet Tom

The battle is not won on the battlefield; it is won in the planning room. An experienced military general will tell you that battles are not won on the battlefield. It is in the army general's office, before any battle takes place, that strategies are formed and battles are won. Experienced generals spend significant time studying the enemy's strengths and weaknesses, as well as the terrain where the battle will be fought.

The army general builds his strategy based on the research invested in the battle. It is better to spend time planning for the battle than to act in haste and lose the battle. The beginning is more important than the end. The introduction matters more than the conclusion. You need to persuade the reader from the beginning so they will continue to read and explore your story. Therefore, I have carefully what to write at the outset The incredible power and mystery of the Bible are evident in its beginnings. As you read the story of creation in Genesis, you are captivated by the account.

What an incredible story and what a great way to start such a complex subject on how it all began. Who is this God we are talking about? How does He present Himself in the beginning? The author of Genesis, though inspired by divine providence and power, provides an explanation of creation that no human mind could fully grasp.

Every time I read the story of the creation; I am continually amazed by God's wonders. The story is woven with such simplicity yet a profound complexity that anyone can understand without the story losing its depth and magnificence. A simple person can be touched by it, yet a university professor or renowned theologian can grapple with its complexity and be awed by its depth. The story of the beginning captivates us, and if we are engaged at the start, we are likely to be compelled to reach the conclusion.

Thanks be to God, who has blessed us with every spiritual blessing in the heavenly places in Christ Jesus. As we begin this journey, we need to understand two keywords to fully comprehend the subject at hand: "secret" and "dominion."

A secret is defined by the Oxford Language Dictionary as something not known or seen by others; hidden or something that is kept unknown or unseen or meant to be kept unknown or unseen by others. The Merriam-Webster dictionary defines a secret as something kept hidden or unexplained, a Mystery, or something kept from knowledge or view of others or shared only confidentially with a few.

This book, therefore, deals with the subject of the secret of achieving dominion. Are you excited about discovering something that is supposed to be unknown? Something that is hidden will be revealed to you. Something hidden will be revealed to you. What a great moment to know what is unknown. What a great moment it is to uncover what is unknown! It is a secret that will change your life forever. Be prepared to be empowered, and set aside everything else to focus on what is written in this book. Those who seek to know a secret must demonstrate readiness and regard what is given as important.

God takes pleasure in revealing what is unknown to His children. When He was about to destroy Sodom and Gomorrah, He said, "Shall I hide from Abraham what I am doing?" (Gen. 18.17). Amos 3:7 says, "Surely the Lord GOD does nothing, unless He reveals His secret to His servants the prophets." This is the nature of God; He wants His secrets about life to be known to His people. In Jeremiah 33:3 the word of the lord says "Call to Me, and I will answer you, and show you great and mighty things, which you do not know."

Wow, what a promise from God! What a desire that the potter would love to see the clay come to know the secret, of how it can be moulded to be the perfect vessel God desires. In Luke 8:17, Luke the physician reveals, "For nothing is secret that will not be revealed, nor anything hidden that will not be known and come to light."

You see God's intent: He desires to reveal the secret of how to have dominion and fulfill the purposes He has for your life. God, who is all-knowing, wants what is hidden in the spiritual realm to be made known to man so that he can take command of his environment and exert influence and dominion in a given territory. Deuteronomy 29:29 clearly states, "The secret things belong to the LORD our God, but those things which are revealed belong to us and to our children forever, that we may do all the words of this law." God reveals His secrets to man to enable him to fulfill his purpose and mandate, as seen in Genesis 1:26-28. God truly and honestly desire that His children have dominion over every situation that confronts them. In Luke 10:19, Jesus says, "Behold, I give you the authority to trample on serpents and scorpions, and over all the power of the enemy, and nothing shall by any means hurt you." You have absolute power or dominion over their demonic or satanic powers. You must reign for his glory.

What then is dominion? This dominion which God spoke about when He created Man; what is it? What is its purpose? How can one achieve it? The Oxford Language Dictionary defines dominion as sovereignty or control, the power or right of governing and controlling, or sovereign authority. In dominion, we see images of power, control, and the right of authority. God has given man power and authority to control certain circumstances in his life and to manifest the sovereignty of God and His story. You, therefore, have the right to rise up and take total control of the prevailing situations in your life. God has given you the power to bring circumstances into subjection so that you display the splendour and glory of God in all you do.

Let's consider the story of Daniel in the fiery furnace. What do you see? You see a man who has absolute dominion and control over his environment, and the outcome is that the king recognized that the God of Daniel was the true God. The power and authority displayed by Daniel in that dire situation changed the king's mindset and ultimately impacted the entire empire. In this book, you will learn the secrets of how to have power and authority to display the splendour of God's glory. Are you ready? The following pages and chapters will offer you insights into how you can achieve this. What are you waiting for? Turn the pages and discover these secrets to transform your life.

2

Reflections

"Reflection gives the brain an opportunity to pause amidst the chaos, untangle and sort through observations and experiences, consider multiple possible interpretations, and create meaning" -Anonymous

"Look, you are here. Do not act like nothing has happened."
— Prophet Tom Tirivangani

Wise and Foolish Builders

Life is not a product of random chance but the outcome of deliberate and intentional planning and execution of goals and objectives. You will have to make a choice, a wise choice, for that matter, on how you are going to reach your goal and fulfill the purpose of your life. The teaching of Jesus about who is a wise builder and who is a foolish builder is an appropriate starting point.

Are you a WISE builder or a FOOLISH builder? There is nothing like, "I AM JUST A BUILDER." Jesus's teaching in Mathew 7:24- 29 shows us that our choices will either make us wise builders or foolish builders. In life you can either become bitter or better, it is a matter of choice.

> Therefore, everyone who hears these words of mine and puts them into practice is like a wise man who built his house on the rock. The rain came down, the streams rose, and the winds blew and beat against that house; yet it did not fall, because it had its foundation on the rock. But everyone who hears these words of mine and does not put them into practice is like a foolish man who built his house on sand. The rain came down, the streams rose, and the winds blew and beat against that house, and it fell with a great crash." When Jesus had finished saying these things, the crowds were amazed at his teaching because he taught as one who had authority, and not as their teachers of the law. (Matt. 7.24-29, NIV)

Is there such a thing as someone who can prepare to live a victorious life? Can you really avoid failure?

Good morning to you, believer. I believe that the reason why you are reading this book about the secrets of achieving dominion is because you want to mature and be ready for a new level in life. You want something that can help you achieve that. You are holding an incredible book that will transform your life. You will never be the same again after reading this book. These are not the words of man but of the Holy Spirit because I never write anything unless God ordains it. This is a book ordained by God for his children.

Preparation is a broad subject, and we cannot cover everything in this book. We are specifically concerned with spiritual preparation. As you read this book, do not just read it. Do it prayerfully. The words contained here are not simple words but spiritual words. They are words of the spirit of Jesus Christ. These words are meant to transform those who hear them so that they may be like Jesus Christ. Many people make the big mistake of trying to understand Spiritual things using the carnal or natural mind. There is a vast difference between the spiritual world and the natural world.

In the story of Lazarus and the rich man in Luke 16.26, Father Abraham said, "And besides all this, between us and you there is a great gulf fixed, so that those who want to pass from here to you cannot, nor can those from there pass to us." This is the mystery God has made in such a way that spiritual things can only be understood by Spiritual people. The chaos we see in this world is the error of man trying to understand spiritual things with natural minds. In 1 Corinthians 2.14 (NIV), we read: "The person without the Spirit does not accept the things that come from the Spirit of God but considers them foolishness, and cannot understand them because they are discerned only through the Spirit." The natural world or the natural state of man is inferior to the spiritual state of man. Spiritual maturity is a subject of the spiritual world, and therefore only those who have become spiritually mature are able to understand this subject.

I have studied many books to understand the meaning of life. I became an avid reader and a committed lifelong student. I have always been troubled by ignorance. I have always wanted to be in charge of my environment. I hate to wake up in the morning and not know what to do. God said in Jeremiah 29.11 (NIV), "For I KNOW the plan I have for you." Do I have a plan for my future? What am I doing to plan ahead? Most Christians are stuck on, "As the spirit leads." I have read the bible over and over again and I have discovered that God plans EVERYTHING. NOTHING, absolutely NOTHING just happens randomly. Somewhere, somehow, God planned the event. Before Abraham became a father of many nations, God planned it. God set Abraham on a path that would make him successful. God planned and orchestrated the deliverance of the people of Israel from bondage. It appears God had forgotten because four hundred and thirty years had passed without reprieve. God's people suffered more and more. In a dramatic turn of events, God's plan became evident. God did this by unrolling His plan to save a Hebrew boy called Moses while other children were killed because he wanted to use Moses to deliver his people from bondage in Egypt. God is a MASTER PLANNER. The wisdom of God is incomparable.

In the journey of understanding the purpose of my life and in pursuit of my destiny, I have searched everywhere and sought to acquire knowledge to understand how a man could know his future to help him live the life God intended him to live. I was sick and tired of seeing people live their lives as if they were a product of random chance. I knew in my heart that God was in control, and if God was in control, He surely wanted me for sure to be in control of my life. As a Father, he loves to watch me navigate the journey of my destiny, like a good father who has taken his son to a swimming pool. A Father who wants to see his son in charge in the waters. God does not want us to fear the waters of life. Rather, God delights to see us gliding in the waters of life and being in charge. When God created man in His image and likeness, God said, "Have Dominion." In other words, be in charge of the vast host of the arrays of the earth. God did not want the environment to dominate His children. God wanted His children to dominate the environment and to use their God-given gifts and abilities to do this. Sadly, in today's Christian world, it seems not to be the case. Watching born-again Christians is sad and heartbreaking. In Mark 6.32-34, Jesus watched His followers. They were like sheep without a shepherd. "So they departed to a deserted place in the boat by themselves. But the multitudes saw them departing, and many knew Him and ran there on foot from all the cities. They arrived before them and came together to Him. And Jesus, when He came out, saw a great multitude and was moved with compassion for them, because they were like sheep not having a shepherd. So He began to teach them many things." (Mark 6.32-34).

I sought to understand what "sheep without a shepherd" meant. What did Jesus see in them? Jesus himself is the Good Shepherd. In John 10.11 – 13 Jesus said, "I am the good shepherd. The good shepherd gives His life for the sheep. But a hireling, he who is not the shepherd, one who does not own the sheep, sees the wolf coming and leaves the sheep and flees; and the wolf catches the sheep and scatters them. The hireling flees because he is a hireling and does not care about the sheep." Jesus knew what it meant to be a good shepherd. The good shepherd watches over the sheep and directs them. This was not so with this group of people. They were people who had no vision. They did not know where they were going. They had no shepherd to lead them. They were vulnerable to the savage wolves of Christ's day. The wolves were men and women who were unwilling to spare the flock. They distorted the truth and confused the flock. They made themselves visible and important and Christ, the true Shepherd, is pushed to the sidelines. They took center stage. But in today's church, although these Evil and satanic prophets appropriate everything for themselves, they are unable to lead the flock. Year after year, the flock has no direction or vision. These prophets are unable to make a sacrifice to seek the face of God and inquire on behalf of the flock, which way the flock ought to go. These evil teachers and prophets attract people with their cleverly devised stories.

> But there was a certain man called Simon, who previously practiced sorcery in the city and astonished the people of Samaria, claiming that he was someone great, to whom they all gave heed, from the least to the greatest, saying, "This man is the great power of God." And they heeded him because he had astonished them with his sorceries for a long time. But when they believed Philip as he preached the things concerning the kingdom of God and the name of Jesus Christ, both men and women

> were baptized. Then Simon himself also believed; and when he was baptized he continued with Philip, and was amazed, seeing the miracles and signs which were done. (Acts 8.9-13)

Christ wants to counter the activities of occultic teachers and prophets who mislead people. Christ wants us to stand on His behalf as the Good Shepherd to the flock and lead His flock in the path of righteousness for His name's sake. Sadly, the prophetic ministry has been invaded by savage wolves in sheep's clothing. Apostle Paul warned the elders of the Ephesus church as he was going to Jerusalem. He was convicted that this was the last time they would see him because prophetic messages had been given that Apostle Paul would be arrested in Jerusalem. At the risk of his personal safety, Apostle Paul wanted to continue with his assignment. This is the message he gave to the elders of the church:

> Therefore I testify to you this day that I am innocent of the blood of all men. For I have not shunned to declare to you the whole counsel of God. Therefore take heed to yourselves and to all the flock, among which the Holy Spirit has made you overseers, to shepherd the church of God which He purchased with His own blood. For I know this, that

> after my departure savage wolves will come in among you, not sparing the flock. Also from among yourselves men will rise up, speaking perverse things, to draw away the disciples after themselves. Therefore watch, and remember that for three years I did not cease to warn everyone night and day with tears. (Acts 20:26-31)

The prophetic message given by Paul seemed to have been intended for the local assembly at Ephesus at that time. As a century has passed, it is clear that the message of the man of God was profound. It was a clear warning to the universal church, the body of Christ. Today, everyone who truly loves God can see the savage wolves at work, sometimes working harder than the true servants of God. We must be on guard. We must be ready to fight to protect the flock.

Centuries before the birth of Jesus Christ, King David knew the importance of a shepherd. The true Shepherd was and is God. This is the eternal and universal truth. In a state of deep reflection on how God had led him and protected him during the time he spent shepherding his father's flock, he wrote a moving Psalms, the famous Psalms 23. This is what King David had to say in the first few verses of that Psalms: "The Lord is my shepherd; I shall not want. He makes me to lie down in green pastures; He leads me beside the still waters. He restores my soul; He leads me in the paths of righteousness For His name's sake. (Ps. 23.1-3)

The will of God is laid bare in these passages of scripture. God wants to direct our steps. The steps of a righteous man are ordered by the Lord. Therefore, nobody can understand the secret of achieving dominion without knowing what to expect. But this does not just happen by chance. This is the time for those who are called as leaders in the body of Christ to stand in prayer, seeking the face of God so that they may be able to direct the flock. Thomas, the disciple of Jesus, often regarded as doubting Thomas, asked Jesus a very important question: "Lord, we do not know where You are going, and how can we know the way?" (John 14.5) Biblical scholars have often glossed over the contribution made by Thomas to the Christian faith. Without Thomas's question, we might never know the important truth. In response to his question, "Jesus said to him, "I am the way, the truth, and the life. No one comes to the Father except through Me."(John 14.6). This was an astounding and outstanding declaration that was ever made by any man. This is the foundation of the Christian faith: Jesus Christ is the WAY. There is no other way except through Christ. Jesus Christ's message was clear, unambiguous and unequivocal: "I AM HE."

Our generation has lacked a group of teachers and prophets who have the clout and insight to guide the flock. Instead, the prophets and teachers of our time have largely contributed to the maze of confusion we see in the body of Christ. Many Christians are filled with fear, doubt and worry. FEAR seems to have taken over almost everyone, everywhere. We cannot enjoy life because fear is everywhere. Fear is the unwanted guest in every family. No matter how many times people tell fear that he is not wanted in their life, FEAR just stubbornly shows up. I have seen how destructive Fear is. Christians seem to be lost. They want to believe, but fear keeps them from believing. You want to belong to a certain church, but fear keeps you from making the decision that you finally have found a home and want to settle down. You keep promising yourself that you will pray to know God's will. When people ask why you have not made the decision, you keep on religiously saying, "I AM PRAYING." Really, the truth is FEAR has kept you from making that decision. It's not that you are praying; the simple truth is that you are JUST AFRAID. There is so much proliferation of false churches and false prophets that Christians are AFRAID to believe that true prophets and living churches exist today. Christians are paralyzed by FEAR. We must conquer this monster called FEAR if we are to live a meaningful life with full dominion.

In this book, I will show you how you can conquer FEAR. You need a new trajectory, a new narrative that God planned our SUCCESS even before we were born. He did not hide the secret from us; "And the disciples came and said to Him, "Why do You speak to them in parables?" He answered and said to them, "Because it has been given to you to know the mysteries of the kingdom of heaven, but to them it has not been given." (Matt. 13.10-11) BORN AGAIN believers are in a unique position. The secret of the things of the Kingdom is with them. God has put them in HIS WORD. If you want to know the secrets, study the word of God. This was the case of Daniel. In Daniel 9, we see how a man who knew that the secrets of the Kingdom of God were hidden in the WORD of God acted:

> In the first year of Darius the son of Ahasuerus, of the lineage of the Medes, who was made king over the realm of the Chaldeans— in the first year of his reign I, Daniel, understood by the books the number of the years specified by the word of the Lord through Jeremiah the prophet, that He would accomplish seventy years in the desolations of Jerusalem. Then I set my face toward the Lord God to make request by prayer and supplications, with fasting, sackcloth, and ashes. (Daniel 9:1-3)

There are a few questions that keep on coming to everyone: Can someone know what path to take in their life and avoid the hit-and-miss spiritual syndrome? Does God want you to have a successful life? Does God care what happens to your life? There are 7.8 billion people in the world today; how does God care about me in the midst of such a great multitude of people? I am not famous. I am not important. Not many people know me in my community. In my small community, people keep asking me, "Who are you, by the way? What's your name again?" These are some of the challenging questions we face every day in life. Biblical figures faced the same questions at their time. When the angel appeared to Gideon in Judges 6:12 and greeted him "...Mighty man of Valor," Gideon was shocked. He might have asked himself, "Me, a mighty man of Valor? Are you kidding me?" It seems a fairytale, But this story is true. You will have to read this story in the book of Judges to understand what I am saying. I will save you time by providing you with the story here.

> Now the Angel of the Lord came and sat under the terebinth tree which was in Ophrah, which belonged to Joash the Abiezrite, while his son Gideon threshed wheat in the winepress, in order to hide it from the Midianites. And the Angel of the Lord appeared to him, and said to him, "The Lord is with you, you mighty man of valor!" Gideon said to Him, "O my lord, if the Lord is with us, why then has all this happened to us? And where are all His miracles which our fathers told us about, saying, 'Did not the Lord bring us up from Egypt?' But now the Lord has forsaken us and delivered us into the hands of the Midianites." Then the Lord turned to him and said, "Go in this might of yours, and you shall save Israel from the hand of the Midianites. Have I not sent you?" So he said to

> Him, "O my Lord, how can I save Israel? Indeed my clan is the weakest in Manasseh, and I am the least in my father's house." And the Lord said to him, "Surely I will be with you, and you shall [e]defeat the Midianites as one man." Then he said to Him, "If now I have found favor in Your sight, then show me a sign that it is You who talk with me. Do not depart from here, I pray, until I come to You and bring out my offering and set it before You." And He said, "I will wait until you come back. (Judg. 6.11-18)

Does God really care? Can God wait for me? Who am I that He could wait for me? These are deep and serious life questions. How can we answer them? This book you have just started to read is no ordinary book. It is a book that has been inspired by the Holy Spirit. It contains deep supernatural Knowledge about life in the Kingdom of God. It is Knowledge that, if you had known it before you began the journey of your life, your life could be at another level today. But I believe it's not too late. You can start now with this new walk in life. Take this step seriously. Knowledge is the key that opens closed doors. Knowledge is the compass in your journey of life, and without it, your life has no direction or meaning. The prophet Hosea understood the importance of knowledge. This is reflected in his prophetic writing. In Hosea 4:6, the prophet reveals a deep secret from God: "My people are destroyed for lack of knowledge. Because you have rejected knowledge, I also will reject you from being priest for Me; Because you have forgotten the law of your God, I also will forget your children."

There is no more hunger for knowledge in our generation. We have grown weary. There are no more young men and women who are eager to know God. Who in our generation is sacrificing to discover and build a deeper relationship with God? We are a Microwave generation. We are in a hurry. We can no longer wait for God. We are demanding that God must wait for us. Our new faith is Instagram, Facebook, WhatsApp, whatever you name it; social media has captured our generation. The internet is littered with false stories and false narratives. It's hard to know who to believe. You can photoshop someone's picture and put it together with someone they have never met. It's easy to create a scandal about someone. Just hate them and post a story on social media; it's done. In today's world, you can destroy someone's life just by the PUSH of a BUTTON. Your computer button, your iPhone button is the trigger you can pull and shoot down your ENEMY. The antidote to all of this is, we NEED to TURN to GOD. We need to have a personal relationship with God. We need God in the same way the deer pants for the water. "As the deer pants for the water brooks, So pants my soul for You, O God. (Ps. 41.1)

I challenge you, as you read this book, to read it meditatively. Be clear-headed and intentional. Have a focus and a goal in mind to achieve, then set out relentlessly and fight to reach that goal.

3

Milestones are windows of opportunity

As you embark on this journey of finding dominion, it is important to recognize that you have reached a significant milestone: the milestone of being alive. No dominion can be achieved if you do not first have life. To live from one year to another is a gift and a miracle, a miracle many people take for granted. As I write now, someone has just died or is dying. That person did not make it today, but you did. Are you cleverer than the person who died? Are you better than the one who died? You can stand on your feet; It seems easy, but someone is confined to a wheelchair or has never walked in their life. You can hear with your ears; someone is deaf and wishes they could hear singing birds or even what you call noise. You can see, but someone is saying, "If only I could see, I would never forget what I saw." Often, we take life for granted. How much God spares us every morning has nothing to do with our own goodness. This is the grace of God, and it must not be taken for granted.

The Psalmist David looked at his life and saw the manifold mercies of God. King David stopped and said to himself, "Who am I?" He was overwhelmed and saw the grace of God. In his deep reflection of the manifold grace of God, King David was moved. In that delicate moment, King David wrote one of the most profound reflective statements ever written by a human being: "What shall I return to the Lord for all his goodness to me?" (Ps. 116.12 NIV). This was a statement of a reflective thinker. Life requires reflection if it is to be lived meaningfully, productively, and fruitfully. Life must be lived on purpose and on principle. Your life is not an accident; it is born out of your destiny. Your life is a product of God's thoughtful plan for humanity. In Jeremiah 1.4-5, we encounter this deep thoughtfulness of God: "The word of the Lord came to me, saying, 'Before I formed you in the womb I knew you, before you were born I set you apart; I appointed you as a prophet to the nations'" (Jer. 1:4-5 NIV). This is how profound and thoughtful God is. God cares for each one of us. God knows you by name amid the 7.8 billion people in the world today. Matthew 10:29-31 captures this succinctly: "Are not two sparrows sold for a copper coin? And not one of them falls to the ground apart from your Father's will. But the very hairs of your head are all numbered. Do not fear therefore; you are of more value than many sparrows" (Matt. 10.29-31).

Therefore, your life matters before God. No matter how insignificant one may appear, your life in the eyes of God is very important. It's part of the solution to the puzzle of human life. God created you to be a solution to an aspect of humanity's challenges. But you must also know that in the midst of all this, the devil is busy. The devil wants you to believe that you are nothing, that God does not care about you, that you will not amount to anything, and that you are wasting your time. "See how long you have been trying; has anything changed? Look at your weaknesses. God can't hear a person like you. It's too late. Why don't you just give up?" The devil has managed to deceive many unsuspecting Christians. This has been his decoy since he fell. The devil wants many fallen heroes in our walk of faith. The devil does not get tired; he keeps on looking for a loophole. I want you to see how cunning and deceitful the devil is. The devil is the father of lies. In John 8.44, we get a clear picture of who the devil is: "You belong to your father, the devil, and you want to carry out your father's desires. He was a murderer from the beginning, not holding to the truth, for there is no truth in him. When he lies, he speaks his native language, for he is a liar and the father of lies" (John 8.44 NIV).

See how the holy scriptures describe Satan. Never forget this. God has captured the nature of Satan in His Word. Hear, brothers and sisters, what God says about the devil. Satan is caught and uncovered by the Word of God. He cannot hide from you if you are in the Word of God. As long as you abide in the sacred Word of God, the devil cannot deceive you. The Prophet Hosea in Hosea 4.6 says, "My people are destroyed for lack of knowledge" (Hos. 4.6). It is our ignorance of God's Word that makes us victims of the devil. It is easy for the devil to deceive you if you do not have the Word of God.

The Christians in the first church were a different group of believers. They took the Word of God seriously. They knew the Word of God and sought to apply it to their lives. In Acts 2.42-47, we see how believers who were filled with the Word of God behaved:

> They devoted themselves to the apostles' teaching and to fellowship, to the breaking of bread and to prayer. Everyone was filled with awe at the many wonders and signs performed by the apostles. All the believers were together and had everything in common. They sold property and possessions to give to anyone who had need. Every day they continued to meet together in the temple courts. They broke bread in their homes and ate together with glad and sincere hearts, praising God and enjoying the favor of all the people. And the Lord added to their number daily those who were being saved. (Acts 2.42-47 NIV)

We are told in the beginning of the book of John. 1.1-14, and I paraphrase, "In the beginning was the Word, and the Word was with

God, and the Word was God. And the Word became flesh and dwelt among us." God and His Word are one. God does nothing without His Word. In Paul's letter to the Hebrews, the outstanding man of God repeated and affirmed the power of the Word of God. Apostle Paul said, "For the word of God is living and powerful, and sharper than any two-edged sword" (Heb. 4.12). Your attitude to the Word of God will determine the altitude of your life. He who neglects the Word of God neglects fellowship with God. We can only fellowship with God through His Word. There is no other way to fellowship except by studying His Word.

The Bible gives us another compelling example of believers who loved the Word of God. It was the believers in the city of Berea. The city of Berea was an ancient city in the Hellenistic period and Roman Empire, now known as Veria or Veroia in Macedonia, northern Greece. Berea is a small city on the eastern side of the Vermio mountains, north of Mount Olympus. Although this city was small, the people of this city had a big and amazing attitude towards the Word of God. Acts 17.11-12 is considered to have been authored by St. Luke the physician, who was also the author of the book of Luke, one of the synoptic gospels. He gives a vivid narrative about the believers in the city of Berea. The believers in Berea were quite different from those in Thessalonica. Those in Thessalonica were arrogant and argumentative. The Word of God did not have a place in their hearts. These men and women who claimed to be believers did not reflect a community that lived in the Word of God. Instead, they enjoyed debate and controversy. They opposed Apostle Paul and created commotion for him in the name of the Lord. The devil had captured their minds. But not so with the Bereans. The writer tells us: "These were more fair-minded than those in Thessalonica, in that they received the word with all readiness, and searched the Scriptures daily to find out whether these things were so. Therefore many of them believed, and also not a few of the Greeks, prominent women as well as men" (Acts 17.11-12).

Do you sometimes find yourself to be like a Thessalonian believer? Argumentative, fault-finding, an accuser of brethren, yet claiming to be a born-again believer? You are tearing apart the body of Christ instead of building it. You are living in sin, yet you accuse your brothers and sisters. You have no fruit of the Spirit, no fruit of righteousness, yet you claim to be knowledgeable in the Word of God. You claim to be a teacher and a minister of the Word of God, yet you are full of selfish ambition, jealousy, envy, and hatred. Such knowledge is sensual and evil. It does not come from the Word of God, neither does it come from God Almighty, the Father of lights.

Many Christians today have fallen victim to the devil because they do not have the Word of God. Many Christians have fallen victim to deceptive prophets who are agents of the devil because they do not have the Word of God. Most Christians do not have a habit of reading and studying the Word of God. Those who have managed to develop a habit of reading the Word do not read it accurately. They have the scriptures in their heads, but they do not have the life of the scriptures. In other words, they have religious knowledge of the scripture but not spiritual knowledge of the scripture.

In the time of our Lord Jesus, there was a group of religious scholars and teachers who were trapped by this issue. They were called Pharisees, scribes, and Sadducees. Even the council of the Sanhedrin fell victim to this. They continuously accused our Lord Jesus of breaking the law, yet, in their religious knowledge of the Word of God, their way of living was the complete opposite of the Word they purported to support and teach.

Therefore, brothers and sisters, when you read the scriptures, do not just read for the sake of reading. Read to connect with Jesus Christ. In the same way, we have many believers today who have scripture, yet they do not have the life offered in the scripture. They are dead inside; their lives do not reflect the scripture they have crammed in their heads. The scriptures are not living in them. They are full of hatred, jealousy, evil speech, and full of lust. These believers are stuck in religion. They have the form of godliness but deny the power of the Word of God. I pray this does not sound like you.

From the first fall in the Garden of Eden, the cause of the fall was the lack of knowledge of the Word, even between Adam and Eve. Although Adam and Eve had it all in the Garden of Eden, they lost it all in just one day. In that same garden, they had fellowship with God in the cool of the day. They lost the Word and then lost fellowship.

It is possible for you as a believer to lose it all if you lose the Word of God. Let's examine the story of Adam and Eve's fall in the Garden. How did Satan manage to manipulate Eve, the mother of all human beings, who in turn corrupted Adam, the first man and father of all human beings? Let's see what happened. Perhaps we could learn many lessons from this story.

Below are the key aspects of the story after God had created man and put him in the Garden:

In Genesis 2.15-17, it is recorded: "Then the Lord God took the man and put him in the garden of Eden to tend and keep it. And the Lord God commanded the man, saying, "Of every tree of the garden you may freely eat; but of the tree of the knowledge of good and evil you shall not eat, for in the day that you eat of it you shall surely die."

God's message was quite simple. It was not complex. God had a message to Adam: "I have put you in the garden to take care of it. Eat everything but do not eat from the tree of knowledge of good and evil. If you eat from it, you will die." This was the simplest message I have ever heard in my life. But although the message was simple, it contained the profound mystery of being God's first divine instruction in righteousness to man.

What then happened? How did the devil manage to twist the message and deceive Eve? In Genesis 3, we see the manipulation of the devil. This has been his method and scheme of attacking gullible and ignorant Christians.

Now the serpent was more cunning than any beast of the field which the Lord God had made. And he said to the woman, 'Has God indeed said, "You shall not eat of every tree of the garden?"' And the woman said to the serpent, 'We may eat the fruit of the trees of the garden; but of the fruit of the tree which is in the midst of the garden, God hath said, "You shall not eat it, nor shall you touch it, lest you die."' Then the serpent said to the woman, 'You will not surely die. For God knows that in the day you eat of it your eyes will be opened, and you will be like God, knowing good and evil.' (Gen. 3.1-5)

A deep study and reflection reveal how the devil wins many people to himself. He introduces a lie to a Christian who does not have the Word of God in their heart. He wants to portray God as harsh and unloving. "Did God really say you must not eat from any tree in the garden? If God is loving, how can He bar you from eating from any tree in the garden?" However, Genesis 2.16 shows that God never said that. It was the devil who invented the story in his attempt to twist the truth. Eve's answer shows a glaring lack of knowledge of God's Word. What Eve was saying was not what God said to Adam. Eve was simply ignorant of what God said to Adam. Eve said, "We may eat fruit from the trees in the garden, but God said you must not eat fruit from the tree in the midst of the garden, and you must not touch it, or you will die." Where did Eve get the idea that they were not to eat from the tree in the middle of the garden or touch it? A reading of Genesis 2.16 shows that Eve did not have the Word of God. Satan used that loophole to attack Adam and Eve. Suddenly, the people who had it all lost it all.

Many Christians rely on hearsay. They never take the time to study the Word of God for themselves. I have been shocked at times when I hear Christians say, "The Bible says this or that," and I wonder where they got that from. No, the Bible never said that. When I was growing up as a Catholic, we never read the Bible. We relied on what the priest said. If he missed it, we all missed it. The believers in Berea did the opposite. They studied the Word of God. The story of the fall reflects how dangerous it is for a Christian to live without a true knowledge of the Word of God. The Apostle Paul was aware of this scheme and modus operandi of the devil, as he warned the young Bishop Timothy. In 2 Timothy 2.15, Paul exhorted Timothy by saying: "Be diligent to present yourself approved to God, a worker who does not need to be ashamed, rightly dividing the word of truth."

He urged Timothy to study the Word of God so that he could have a proper and sound understanding of it. Paul wanted Timothy to be able to properly interpret the Word of God and teach it to the people of God.

The devil is real and was real in the time of Paul. Paul knew that the devil was ready to exploit any gaps or ignorance of the Word of God. All the apostles were vigilant and had a clear understanding that the devil was a wicked and deceptive creature who should never be given a foothold in anyone's life. Sensing a great danger to the church, Peter exhorted the believers throughout the provinces of Pontus, Galatia, Cappadocia, Asia, and Bithynia to "Be sober, be vigilant; because your adversary the devil walks about like a roaring lion, seeking whom he may devour" (1 Pet. 5.8).

The devil is angry because he was cast down to the earth. This story is recorded in Revelation 12.7-9: "And war broke out in heaven: Michael and his angels fought with the dragon; and the dragon and his angels fought, but they did not prevail, nor was a place found for them in heaven any longer. So the great dragon was cast out, that serpent of old, called the Devil and Satan, who deceives the whole world; he was cast to the earth, and his angels were cast out with him" (Rev. 12.7-9).

In that battle, the devil was defeated and humiliated. He lost everything and was defeated by the archangel Michael. Today, the devil is even angrier because he was ultimately destroyed by Christ. When Christ was crucified, died, and was buried, He did the unimaginable. He descended into the lower regions of the earth (hell) and took captive Satan and his cohorts. He made them a public spectacle. He humiliated Satan and triumphed over him through His death and resurrection:

> And you, being dead in your trespasses and the uncircumcision of your flesh, He has made alive together with Him, having forgiven you all trespasses, having wiped out the handwriting of requirements that was against us, which was contrary to us. And He has taken it out of the way, having nailed it to the cross. Having disarmed principalities and powers, He made a public spectacle of them, triumphing over them in it. (Colossians 2:13-15)

Now Satan is looking for revenge. He wants to destroy many and lead many Christians to the judgment seat of Christ. But I want you to know the good news. The good news is that Satan has no power over your life. No matter what temptation Satan may bring against your life, Jesus Christ has provided a way out of that temptation. The secret lies in hiding the Word of God in your heart. David said, "Your word I have hidden in my heart, that I might not sin against You" (Psalm 119.11). The weapon of both attack and defense is God's Word.

In 1 Corinthians 10.13, the Apostle Paul reminds us, "No temptation has overtaken you except such as is common to man; but God is faithful, who will not allow you to be tempted beyond what you are able, but with the temptation will also make the way of escape, that you may be able to bear it."

It is clear from the Scriptures that no matter what weapon Satan might use to tempt, we have only one weapon to fight back. It's the Word of God. It's that simple and powerful. Yet it is the simple truth that is missed by many people. When we examine the life of Jesus, we see this principle at work. Our Lord and Savior was filled with the Word of God. He is the Word of God Himself. The temptation of Jesus in the wilderness is a dramatic and profound story of a cunning and deceitful enemy, Satan, determined and desperate to mislead, but was wisely defeated by our Savior, Jesus Christ. This is recorded in Matthew 4.1-11:

> Then Jesus was led up by the Spirit into the wilderness to be tempted by the devil. And when He had fasted forty days and forty nights, afterward He was hungry. Now when the tempter came to Him, he said, 'If You are the Son of God, command that these stones become bread.' But He answered and said, 'It is written, "Man shall not live by bread alone, but by every word that proceeds from the mouth of God."' Then the devil took Him up into the holy city, set Him on the pinnacle of the temple, and said to Him, 'If You are the Son of God, throw Yourself down. For it is written: "He shall give His angels charge over you," and, "In their hands they shall bear you up, lest you dash your foot against a stone."' Jesus said to him, 'It is written again, "You shall not tempt the Lord your God."' Again, the devil took Him up on an exceedingly high mountain, and showed Him all the kingdoms of the world and their glory. And he said to Him, 'All these things I will give You if You will fall down and worship me.' Then Jesus said to him, 'Away with you, Satan! For it is written, "You shall worship the Lord your God, and Him only you shall serve."' Then the

devil left Him, and behold, angels came and ministered to Him. (Matt. 4.1-11)

A serious reflection on the story of the temptation of Jesus Christ in the wilderness reveals that our mightiest weapon against the schemes of the devil is God's Word. God and His Word are one. "In the beginning was the Word, and the Word was with God, and the Word was God" (John 1:1). Standing in the Word gives us the assurance of complete victory over the devil.

The temptation of Jesus Christ in the wilderness is one of the most remarkable stories that demonstrates the power in the Word of God. From the first temptation to the last, the devil tried every trick in his wicked scheme and philosophy to tempt the Son of God. The answer to each question and attack by the devil was met with a firm conviction in the power of the Word of God. Jesus replied to the devil at every turn by saying, "It is written." These are not simple words. This is not a simple statement. It is a firm declaration that "This is what the Word of God says." What the Word of God says is settled. It is unchangeable and unalterable. This is an unavoidable truth. You either accept it or leave it; that's how it is.

This understanding will give every born-again Christian the power to live a victorious life. It does not matter what happens on the outside. Settled truth has incredible power. Armed with a deep conviction of what God was saying to him, Joseph held on to his dream despite being thrown into the deep and dark dungeon by his brothers. The false accusation of Potiphar's wife and the subsequent imprisonment could not break his resolve and determination to fulfill his destiny. He conveniently reminded himself of this:

Remember Jesus Christ, raised from the dead and descended from David. This is my gospel, for which I suffer trouble as an evildoer, even to the point of chains; but the word of God is not chained. Therefore I endure all things for the sake of the elect, that they also may obtain the salvation which is in Christ Jesus with eternal glory. This is a faithful saying: For if we died with Him, we shall also live with Him. If we endure, we shall also reign with Him. If we deny Him, He also will deny us. If we are faithless, He remains faithful; He cannot deny Himself." (2 Timothy 2:8-13)

The Word of God that had come to him by revelation continued to speak to him, assuring him that despite the confinement of the prison, the best was yet to come. This is Joseph's story of the coat of many colors. It was his revelation of the sheaves of his brothers bowing to his sheaves. No matter what his brothers tried to do, Joseph remained focused. No matter the delay he faced, he kept on believing in his destiny.

What are you going through? What challenges have you been facing? The devil has attacked your life from all sides. You have gone through too much and want to give up. You are thinking of throwing in the towel. What could have happened if Joseph had given up when he was thrown into prison? Joseph chose integrity over the cheap pleasure of sleeping with Potiphar's wife. He knew who he was and what the future held for him.

What about Daniel? Daniel refused the king's delicacies, a shortcut to fulfilling his destiny. He chose the right path. Evil is seductively tempting. As Christians, we are tempted every day to take shortcuts. We want to avoid pain and suffering. What could have happened if Daniel had negotiated his way out of the den of lions or the fiery furnace? What could have happened to humanity if Jesus had called a legion of angels to defend Him so that He would not have to face the cross? Nobody wants pain, and nobody wants to go through pain. But the pain and humiliation we face day-to-day are a necessary foundational course in the university of Jesus Christ. Are you trying to take a shortcut because of what you are going through? Count the cost.

You are given an opportunity to start all over again. The past has been challenging and humiliating. You have suffered and faced disgrace. The devil has tried to rob you of everything, but you have another opportunity. God is the God of another opportunity. What are you going to do now? You can get your life back on track by turning to God. You cannot turn to God without turning to His Word. The Word of God is a lamp unto your feet. By turning to the Word of God, you are turning to God. But you cannot turn to God without turning away from your past. Count your past as over. I mean it's over. Your past is in your past. Consider it done. You cannot move forward while looking back. Nobody ever moved forward while being stuck in the past. Isaiah 43.18-19 captures this, "Do not remember the former things, Nor consider the things of old. Behold, I will do a new thing; Now it shall spring forth; Shall you not know it? I will even make a road in the wilderness And rivers in the desert" (Isa. 43:18-19).

As you prepare to achieve dominion, forgive yourself and forgive others. Do not be stuck in toxic emotions and past hurts. You have been handed an opportunity to start all over again. Do not doubt it. Do not be double-minded. Believe in God's gift to you of a new beginning. It's a new season for you. Embrace it. Do not beat yourself up. That's the trick of the devil to keep you bound under shame, guilt, and condemnation. Your mistakes, no matter how big or terrible, can be corrected. That is the gift of a new beginning. This is what Jesus was saying in Matthew 9:16-17, "No one puts a piece of unshrunk cloth on an old garment; for [e]the patch pulls away from the garment, and the tear is made worse. Nor do they put new wine into old wineskins, or else the wineskins break, the wine is spilled, and the wineskins are ruined. But they put new wine into new wineskins, and both are preserved."

There is no point in trying to achieve dominion and focusing on when the devil deceived you that you did not have dominion. It's not wise, and it does not work, nor does it make your life successful. Stop and reflect. What has brought you this far? What habits brought you pain? What part of your character punched holes in your life? How did you manage your resources? What can you do to help yourself move forward? Remember, the choices you make will either make you or break you. If you make it, it's you; and if you fail, it's you. There is nothing God can do in your life without you. The you in you must be managed properly to allow you a new beginning.

4

Don't Underestimate the Power of Planning

"This is what the Lord says: 'When seventy years are completed for Babylon, I will come to you and fulfill My good promise to bring you back to this place. For I know the thoughts that I think toward you,' says the Lord, 'thoughts of peace and not of evil, to give you a future and a hope. Then you will call upon Me and go and pray to Me, and I will listen to you. And you will seek Me and find Me, when you search for Me with all your heart. I will be found by you,' says the Lord, 'and I will bring you back from your captivity; I will gather you from all the nations and from all the places where I have driven you,' says the Lord, 'and I will bring you to the place from which I caused you to be carried away captive.'" (Jer. 29.10-14)

Planning is one of the most neglected disciplines in the Christian faith, especially among charismatic Pentecostal believers. They prefer the "As the Spirit leads" approach. It is indeed important that the Spirit of Christ must lead. Many years ago, when God called me to full-time ministry, I began to pray and I prayed for months seeking God's guidance. I wanted God to speak to me. I wasn't ready to jump up and start doing things before God gave me a crystal-clear vision. I needed the vision to be clear in my heart. I wanted God to give me the pattern of how I was going to do the ministry. Many Christians have started to run, jumping here and there even before God has finished talking to them. When I had prayed past a year, one day God spoke to me in a powerful audible voice. God said to me, "Tom, this vision is INSPIRED AND LED BY THE SPIRIT OF GOD." From that day forward, I have never done anything unless God inspired it. I have never moved a step forward unless I knew it was the Spirit of God leading me. I made a decision that UNLESS you lead us, God, we will not go. There are times when I have waited for months on matters that appeared simple to everyone else because I wanted the sanction. I know I have offended many people because I refused to do things like everyone else. I have heard others say to me, "Why can't we just do it this way because that's what everyone is doing?" I have said no; it was not about what others were doing, it was about what God wanted us to do. I have resisted people who came with what appeared to be exceptionally good ideas. They genuinely wanted us to succeed, but they were genuinely deceived. What they were giving us were man's ideas. My conviction has always been that it's God's ideas that will make us successful. My deep conviction is, "Let God lead and let man follow." Nothing matters unless it is from God. The Bible reminds us, "Listen to counsel and receive instruction, that you may be wise in your latter days. There are many plans in a man's heart, nevertheless the Lord's counsel—that will stand" (Prov. 19.20-21).

Charismatic Pentecostal believers must, along with being led by the Spirit, learn to plan. When one carefully searches and studies the Holy Scriptures, we will discover, as I have said elsewhere in this book, that God is a Master Planner. God has never allowed anything to be a product of random chance. God had a clear plan before anything was done. A careful study of the creation story recorded in the book of Genesis reveals a recurring statement: "God said, 'Let there be' and there was." So, before anything was created, God had a plan.

Out of that plan, He declared that His plan would come to fruition. In this chapter, we will examine the creation story in detail to see how important planning is if one is going to be successful. After that, I will select what I perceive to be the important aspects of your destiny and how you can plan as you start this journey of achieving dominion.

> In the beginning God created the heavens and the earth. The earth was without form, and void; and darkness was on the face of the deep. And the Spirit of God was hovering over the face of the waters. (Gen. 1.1-2)

The creation story gives a glimpse of how things were before God implemented His plan. In the beginning, the earth was formless, void, and empty, and darkness hovered over the face of the deep. God looked at that and asked, "What can I do to bring form to the earth? What can I do to fix the emptiness? What about the darkness—how can I fix that so there can be light on the face of the earth?" I suppose these are some of the questions God had to ask Himself. He had to have a plan to deal with these challenges. Your life may be formless now; it may be empty and full of darkness. You do not know what to do so that you do not carry the formlessness, emptiness, or darkness that has characterized your life this far into your journey of dominion. You have to sit down or stop and pause to reflect, "What can I do to fix these issues before I ruin my chances of achieving dominion?" Unless you strategically stop and reflect on where you are and where you are going, you are sure to ruin the opportunity God has presented you by giving you the gift of a NEW START. When we go back to the story, we see something incredible that God did. "Then God said, 'Let there be light'; and there was light. And God saw the light, that it was good; and God divided the light from the darkness. God called the light Day and the darkness He called Night. So the evening and the morning were the first day" (Gen. 1.3-5).

You see, God had a plan to deal with the darkness. He turned the darkness into light by implementing His plan. God did not stop there; He continued with His PLAN of ACTION. Light did not just come by chance; it was a revelation of God's plan. Do you have a revelation and a plan on how you are going to deal with the darkness that has covered your life? The darkness may be your struggle with adultery and sexual immorality, jealousy, envy, hatred, self-ambition, or pride. These weaknesses will not just go away by themselves. You can't just wish them away. You need to have a plan on how to deal with them. Sit down and set goals to address the darkness that confronts your life. Satan is a deceptive creature; unless you are careful, he will seductively sneak your old habits into the new path of achieving dominion to ruin it. Do not allow the devil to do this. God did not stop just with the LIGHT.

> And God said, "Let the waters under the heavens be gathered together into one place, and let the dry land appear." And it was so. And God called the dry land Earth, and the gathering together of the waters He called Seas. And God saw that it was good. Then God said, "Let the earth bring forth grass, the herb that yields seed, and the fruit tree that yields fruit according to its kind, whose seed is in itself, on the earth." And it was so. And the earth brought forth grass, the herb that yields seed according to its kind, and the tree that yields fruit, whose seed is in itself according to its kind. And God saw that it was good. So the evening and the morning were the third day. (Gen. 1.9-13)

When the darkness was removed, it was clear that the land was dry and barren. God did not want to see dryness and barrenness, and He said, "Let there be water, and let the land be fruitful and productive." In the same way, God does not want dryness and barrenness in your life. God wants your destiny to be fruitful and productive. What are you doing to ensure that your life does not continue to be barren? In John 15:8, Jesus said, "By this My Father is glorified, that you bear much fruit; so you will be My disciples." God's plan for you is that He wants you to be fruitful.

There is a secret that most Christians miss. This is the reason why many Christians are either dead spiritually or merely religious. The creation story reveals the deep secrets of the Kingdom of God. When you examine this story, you will see that God kept on implementing His plan until everything was perfect: "God saw that everything was good." Most Christians stop at one level. If they start praying, they get stuck at one level of prayer. They do not quickly recognize that there are many levels of spiritual growth, maturity, and giving. In the Kingdom of God, there is always another level of commitment. Do not be stuck at one level. That is the most dangerous mistake one can make in their spiritual life. If you allow your life to be stuck on one level, you will either die spiritually or become religious. Christians are created to move from glory to glory in their pursuit of destiny. This is a mindset you must cultivate. In my walk with God, I always believe that the best is yet to come. Develop a deep longing to reach another level in your life. Do not just do things for the sake of doing them. Do not surrender your destiny to mediocrity and chance.

It pleased Darius to set over the kingdom one hundred and twenty satraps, to be over the

> whole kingdom; and over these, three governors, of whom Daniel was one, that the satraps might give account to them, so that the king would suffer no loss. Then this Daniel distinguished himself above the governors and satraps, because an excellent spirit was in him; and the king gave thought to setting him over the whole realm. So the governors and satraps sought to find some charge against Daniel concerning the kingdom; but they could find no charge or fault, because he was faithful; nor was there any error or fault found in him. Then these men said, "We shall not find any charge against this Daniel unless we find it against him concerning the law of his God." (Dan. 6:1-5)

When Daniel was appointed as one of the chief administrators, he decided to distinguish himself. In other words, Daniel made a plan not to be just an ordinary administrator. He planned to be exceptional in his duties. What are you doing in the Kingdom of God? How are you performing your duties? What kind of character and personality do you have? What is your attitude? Have you planned how you want people to see you in the coming year? Are you tired of being mediocre and want to reach another level? As you read this book, my prayer is that your life will never be mediocre. Aim high, strive for excellence, and strive to achieve more. It may be hard, but you can do it. You can be the best. Do not allow challenges, limitations, detours, setbacks, and delays to stop you from dreaming big. God has given you a promise: "I can do all things through Christ who strengthens me"

(Phi. 4:13). The secret to achieving your purpose in life lies in planning.

Many things in life are lost because of a lack of planning. Benjamin Franklin once said, "By failing to prepare, you are preparing to fail." One major cause of failure in life is failing to plan and prepare for what you want to achieve. Few people take planning very seriously. Watch people shopping; you will see that they often shop with their eyes, picking whatever entices them. In most cases, an empty trolley is filled with things they never budgeted for or needed. After returning from the shopping trip, they realize they had more vegetables in the freezer and should not have shopped. After a few weeks, they repeat the same mistake and eventually discard the old food because it has been there for too long. The waste industry receives billions of dollars worth of unused food every month. This is why many Christians are poor today. It's not that God does not answer their prayers; they simply can't plan and manage. The majority of those who plan do not execute and implement their plans. I have experienced this in my life—often, we plan to do something, but we end up doing what we did not plan. Planning cannot, of course, be the panacea for all problems, but studies have shown that planning eliminates most causes of failure in life.

The biggest mistake one can make in life is to believe that life is a matter of chance. Those who believe so will either end up nowhere or become frustrated and give up. The Bible, from Genesis to Revelation, offers a different conclusion. God plans, and nothing happens by chance. Those who are successful are good planners. When they plan, they follow through by implementing their plans. Great achievers are great planners. What plan are you putting in place as you are about to start your journey to achieving dominion? Once the plan is set, the next important thing for you as a believer is to set goals for what you want to achieve. What do you want to achieve for the remainder of this year, what do you want to achieve for next year? Do not leave the year blank. The year must be filled with goals for each month, each quarter, and for the year. Dan Clark says, "Goal setting is the strongest force for human motivation. Set a goal and make it true." As a believer, you play a critical role in setting the direction of your destiny. Setting achievable goals is as critical as having a heart in your body. If the heart is not there or is not beating or functioning, there is no life. Goals must neither be too big nor too small. You need the right size for everything. Henry Ford wrote, "Nothing is particularly difficult if you break it into small parts."

The way you think is especially important. With the right thinking, three-quarters of the work is done. One percent of wrong thinking can ruin an entire destiny. Therefore, your mindset matters. Proverbs 23.7 says, "For as he thinks in his heart, so is he." We are what we think. We accomplish extraordinarily little with a mentality that we cannot. The life of a believer can only be transformed if their mind is renewed (Rom. 12.2). Great accomplishments are achieved by those who believe they can. The "Yes, we can" mindset took Barack Obama to the Presidency of the United States of America and the White House. This was a remarkable feat for the first African American to occupy that office. You too can make history. It's the mindset that needs to shift. When you shift your mindset, you are able to shift your destiny.

5

God First: Prioritizing Your Relationship with Him

Are you truly born again? Are you walking in the light? Do you realize how much you need God? Your relationship with God is your security and guarantee for achieving dominion fully. No matter what you have gone through in the past, God wants you to rise up again. Isaiah 60.1-5 tells us, "Arise, shine; For your light has come! And the glory of the Lord is risen upon you. For behold, the darkness shall cover the earth, And deep darkness the people; But the Lord will arise over you, And His glory will be seen upon you. The Gentiles shall come to your light, And kings to the brightness of your rising. "Lift up your eyes all around, and see: They all gather together, they come to you; Your sons shall come from afar, And your daughters shall be nursed at your side. Then you shall see and become radiant, And your heart shall swell with joy; Because the abundance of the sea shall be turned to you, The wealth of the Gentiles shall come to you." Your relationship with God is the catalyst to your destiny.

How can you rise up? What do you need to do? The promises of God are true and firm. It is your time to arise. Your destiny has been in the valley of dry bones for a long time. You did not know how you could get out of this dark place in your life. Ezekiel found himself doubting and unsure of how the dry bones he saw would live again. The word of the Lord came and commanded him to speak to the dry bones. The power of life and death is in the tongue. Spoken words have creative power. The spoken word has an anointing to create something out of nothing. But you need to "speak the word." Do not speak your own ideas but speak the word of the Lord. The secret is in your mouth, as Moses wrote in Deuteronomy 30:11-14: "For this commandment which I command you today is not too mysterious for you, nor is it far off. It is not in heaven, that you should say, 'Who will ascend into heaven for us and bring it to us, that we may hear it and do it?' Nor is it beyond the sea, that you should say, 'Who will go over the sea for us and bring it to us, that we may hear it and do it?' But the word is very near you, in your mouth and in your heart, that you may do it."

In order for you to speak the word of God in faith, you need a relationship with God. God reveals His secret in John 15. 5-8, "I am the vine; you are the branches. He who abides in Me, and I in him, bears much fruit; for without Me you can do nothing. If anyone does not abide in Me, he is cast out as a branch and is withered; and they gather them and throw them into the fire, and they are burned. If you abide in Me, and My words abide in you, you will ask what you desire, and it shall be done for you. By this My Father is glorified, that you bear much fruit; so you will be My disciples."

When you are connected to the life-giver, Jesus Christ, the very life of Christ will feed your destiny and give you the power and anointing to stand up and pursue God's purpose for your life. The more you allow the word of God to inhabit your life, the greater the opportunity to release the potential within you. That potential lies in the seed of your born-again experience. Being born again is the most wonderful thing a person can experience in their life. Every born-again experience infuses the believer with the seed of victory. You cannot be born again and remain the same; for the bible tells us, "For whatever is born of God overcomes the world. And this is the victory that has overcome the world—our faith. Who is he who overcomes the world, but he who believes that Jesus is the Son of God?" (1 John 5.4-5).

Faith is a powerful weapon—a real weapon that one must hold onto. The great heroes of faith in the Bible were men and women of great faith who had a deep, intimate relationship with God. Paul was beaten, imprisoned, and persecuted because he sought to develop an unshakable relationship with Jesus Christ. History records that the Apostle John was beaten, thrown into a drum of boiling oil, and left for dead on the island of Patmos, yet he refused to renounce his relationship with Christ. John knew that apart from Christ, he could do nothing. You need a real connection with Christ for you to be fruitful and acceptable to the Lord.

God is a God of order. Before the Lord does anything, He sets things in a decent and orderly way. In 1 Kings 18:30-38 we saw that before Elijah could call fire from heaven, the prophet prepared the altar and put things in order.

To achieve dominion, a believer needs to be thoughtful and careful. A careful and calculated plan is necessary for an individual believer to reach their goal and destiny. Setting your spiritual life in order is a key aspect of preparing to achieve dominion. How could you achieve dominion without God's order? Everyone needs the backing of God, but before you step out to act and activate your faith in God, you cannot just step out impulsively. You need to pause, think, reflect and then act. Have you spent time—sufficient time—with God?

Spending quiet time with God in prayer and meditation is indispensable. God wants to speak to His children and answer all our prayers. This is God's will in Christ Jesus for you. In Jeremiah 33.3, the Word of God says, "Call to Me, and I will answer you, and show you great and mighty things, which you do not know." God wants to reveal things about our lives that we are unaware of. You see, you are not just what you are. There are aspects of you that, if discovered, would amaze you. You will recognize that beyond your personal struggles lies a great destiny. The reason the devil targets you is because he can see that beyond the temporary setback you are experiencing, you are set up for a comeback. There are several spiritual habits you need to develop to help you realize your dreams in your life. These should be your priority goals to help you reach your future.

God's Will for You

It is easy and tempting to start the year or even search for dominion with our own agenda. We often say, "I want to do this, I want to go there, I want to accomplish this and that." We are tempted to put our will before God's will. This is a tactic of the devil to subvert the will of God, which can be disastrous. Nobody can successfully subvert the will of God. As you begin this journey of seeking dominion, make sure your will aligns with the will of God.

John, the apostle of Jesus Christ and the beloved disciple, was a man whose love for Jesus Christ and conviction was settled. He knew without a shadow of a doubt that believing in Jesus Christ was not just a superficial thing. Fath in Christ is like a revolution; you cannot get connected to it without being changed. Every community that has experienced a revolution has spoken of change and witnessed it. When I came to the faith in Christ Jesus, everything about me changed completely. I became a new creation in Him. It seems John understood this, which is why he wrote, "These things I have written to you who believe in the name of the Son of God, that you may know that you have eternal life and that you may continue to believe in the name of the Son of God. Now this is the confidence that we have in Him, that if we ask anything according to His will, He hears us. And if we know that He hears us, whatever we ask, we know that we have the petitions that we have asked of Him" (1 John 5.13-15).

Our confidence in reaching our destiny does not lie in doing what we want, but in what God has in store for us. We often make New Year resolutions based on our ego, our perception of life and what we think is best for ourselves. Our ego is like a time bomb; a little pressure can ruin our future. Corrie Ten Boom said, "There are no ifs in God's world. And no places that are safer than other places. The center of His will is our safety. Let us pray that we may always know it." Elizabeth Elliot added, "The will of God is not something you add to your life. It's a course you choose. You either line yourself up with the Son of God or capitulate to the principle which governs the rest of the world." The will of God is indeed our safety in a world full of uncertainties. Many people die spiritually because they assume what is good is the will of God. Many things appear good but are not the will of God. Therefore, you need revelation to understand that what is good is not always the will of God. However, we can be assured that God's will is always good for us. As you go on the journey to achieve dominion, make sure you plan to do what God wants you to do.

Instead of telling God what you want to achieve when you have dominion, ask God what He wants from you when you have reached that place of having dominion in your life and the things around you. Remember, many are the plans in a man's heart, but it is the plan of God that will prevail. The best approach for success is to align your will with the will of God. It is a spiritual misstep to order and tell God what you want. God is sovereign, and no one can instruct Him. In Isaiah 40:13-14 (NIV), it says: "Who can fathom the Spirit of the Lord, or instruct the Lord as his counselor? Whom did the Lord consult to enlighten him, and who taught him the right way? Who was it that taught him knowledge, or showed him the path of understanding?"

You may wonder how to know the will of God. Is it possible to know God's will? There is only one sure way to know God's will for you: studying the Word of God. No one can know what God wants without His Word. Studying God's Word must become a daily habit. It's not just reading the Bible; it's about reading it slowly, prayerfully, reverentially, and meditatively. When approached with the right motive, spirit, and understanding, the Bible will reveal the life within its pages. Many teachers of the Word have religious knowledge but lack the life of the Word. In 2013, I met a man who was a professor at a well-known Canadian theological university, responsible for training Bible scholars, pastors, and leaders for over 40 years. After spending two hours discussing the Bible with him and his expertise in the bible, I had a revelation that he lacked the life of the Word despite his PhD in Theology. At the end of our discussion, I asked if he wanted me to pray for him, even though he had already prayed before we began. This ten-minute prayer I offered transformed his life. The heavens opened, the anointing poured out from the throne of heaven and touched his life. The light of Jesus came and illuminated him, leaving him confounded. He was shocked, yet full of joy and tears. He asked how I had done that, because in his 40 years of ministry as a university professor of Theology, he had never experienced such a spiritual encounter. I told him that it was the fruit of properly studying the Word of God. This experience changed his life forever. John 6.63 states, "It is the Spirit who gives life; the flesh profits nothing. The words that I speak to you are spirit, and they are life." As you study the Word of God, ensure you sanctify your motives and read it until the Word becomes life-giving.

6

Dominion Through Prayer and Fasting

Prayer is the key to unlocking the blessings of God in your life. If you want to change your life, you must learn to pray. If you want to live long, you must learn to pray. If you want good health, you must pray for it. If you want to see change in your life, you must learn to pray for it. Prayer gives meaning and direction to your life. It is a lethal weapon against the schemes of Satan. If there is something Satan hates, it is a believer who has learned to pray. Prayer has the power to stop demonic and satanic activity. Where there is prayer, it is difficult for Satan to operate.

Jesus had a lifestyle of prayer. It was His custom to pray. He often woke up early and went to a secluded or lonely place to pray. In Luke 6.12-13 (NIV), we are told that "One of those days Jesus went out to a mountainside to pray, and spent the night praying to God. When morning came, he called his disciples to him and chose twelve of them, whom he also designated apostles." The disciples of Jesus had observed Him praying many times. They had seen John teach his disciples the discipline of prayer. One day the disciples of Jesus approached Him and said, "Lord, teach us to pray, as John also taught his disciples" (Luke 11.1). The disciples suddenly had a deep and compelling conviction about the importance of prayer. They felt a burden surge in their hearts. They knew by revelation of the

Holy Spirit that they needed to know how to pray. They had observed the prayer of the Pharisees, scribes, and Sadducees. It did not impress them; it was ritualistic, monotonous, and filled with vain repetitions. The prayer of Jesus Christ was different; It was deep, compelling, and convicting. It was prayer that was filled with sincerity and love.

Jesus had said to His disciples earlier, "And when you pray, you shall not be like the hypocrites. For they love to pray standing in the synagogues and on the corners of the streets, that they may be seen by men. Assuredly, I say to you, they have their reward. But you, when you pray, go into your room, and when you have shut your door, pray to your Father who is in the secret place; and your Father who sees in secret will reward you openly" (Matt 6.5-6).

It is important that as you read this book, God must give you a burden for prayer. Pray that God will give you a burden to pray like Jesus Christ. Jesus indeed had a compelling burden. The book of Hebrews 5:7 (NIV) captures a deep insight into the manner of Jesus Christ's prayer life: "During the days of Jesus' life on earth, he offered up prayers and petitions with fervent cries and tears to the one who could save him from death, and he was heard because of his reverent submission."

In Habakkuk 2.2, we are told of the burden Habakkuk had: "Then the Lord answered me and said: 'Write the vision and make it plain on tablets, that he may run who reads it.'" In order to pray effectively, one needs a burden. As you prepare to enter into a time of prayer, you must ensure that God has given you a burden. It is the burden that compels you to pray.

Prayer is talking to God, who has the power to change your circumstances. God loves to hear the prayers of His children. Every morning, He waits to hear what His children will say to Him. A break in prayer is a break in communion with God. In Psalms 34.15, "The eyes of the Lord are on the righteous, and His ears are open to their cry."

We are also told in Matthew 7.7-8, "Ask, and it will be given to you; seek, and you will find; knock, and it will be opened to you. For everyone who asks receives, and he who seeks finds, and to him who knocks it will be opened."

There is no doubt that God wants to answer your prayer. In Numbers 23.19, the Word of God says, "God is not a man, that He should lie, nor a son of man, that He should repent. Has He said, and will He not do? Or has He spoken, and will He not make it good?" God is faithful and dependable. When God makes a promise, be sure He will honour His word. The Word of the Lord says God has made Himself a slave to His word; He watches over His word to perform it. In Isaiah 55.11, it is written, "So shall My word be that goes forth from My mouth; it shall not return to Me void, but it shall accomplish what I please, and it shall prosper in the thing for which I sent it."

But why are some of our prayers not answered? You have prayed and prayed, yet you have not received an answer. What is the problem? I can tell you without a shadow of a doubt that God is not the problem. But you say, "I have asked, and God has not answered." Why is it like that if God is so keen to answer my prayer? Many people treat prayer as a ritual and do not take it seriously. They pray haphazardly, lacking wisdom and insight. Effective and productive prayer requires serious preparation and planning. You cannot just jump into prayer and expect God to answer. A lot of people pray out of obligation, which is why their prayers are not answered. They pray randomly and lack understanding. The Word of God provides insight and understanding. It is important to know that your zeal for prayer must be according to knowledge. Effective prayer must be based on the knowledge of the Word of God and also must be inspired by the Holy Spirit. Therefore, careful thought and planning are required if your prayer is to be effective.

In Luke 14:28-32, Jesus said, "For which of you, intending to build a tower, does not sit down first and count the cost, whether he has enough to finish it—lest, after he has laid the foundation and is not able to finish, all who see it begin to mock him, saying, 'This man began to build and was not able to finish'? Or what king, going to make war against another king, does not sit down first and consider whether he is able with ten thousand to meet him who comes against him with twenty thousand? Or else, while the other is still a great way off, he sends a delegation and asks conditions of peace."

As believers and disciples of Jesus Christ, we cannot negotiate with Satan or those in the Satanic kingdom, but the direction of our battle against Satan must be well thought out. This book aims to teach you how to offer effective and powerful prayer that guarantees you victory over Satan every time you pray. Satan is a master deceiver. You must become wiser and shrewder if you are going to defeat him when you enter into prayer. God has given me the ministry and gift of being an intercessor. I am not writing out of mere knowledge; I am writing because I am an intercessor who spends countless hours praying. My life is a life of prayer. I am not telling you what I just know; I am telling you what I know and live. It's what I know and what I do every day. I believe that as you open your heart while reading the words of this book, the fire and burden of prayer will enter into you. There is an impartation taking place as you read this book. Your prayer life will never be the same again. Think again: prayer requires preparation and planning. Do you plan before you pray? Benjamin Franklin reminds us that, "If you fail to plan, you are planning to fail." In Jeremiah 29.11 (NIV) God says, "For I know the plans I have for you." Before God created man, He had a plan for how the man He created would look and what power he would possess. In Genesis 1.26, "Then God said, 'Let Us make man in Our image, according to Our likeness; let them have dominion over the fish of the sea, over the birds of the air, and over the cattle, over all the earth and over every creeping thing that creeps on the earth.'" God had a plan before He created man. He did not create man and then try to develop a plan. Everything was well thought out and put into order by God before it was done. Prayer requires meticulous planning.

In this book, I will show you how to plan for your prayer so that God can answer it. Prayer is a battle. If you have not seen prayer this way, you need to start viewing it as a battle from today. Every time you engage in prayer, two armies are fighting: the army of God on the right and the army of Satan on the left. You are the army general in the army of God directing the battle. You need to sit down and carefully plan how you are going to fight this battle. Remember, prayer requires careful preparation and planning. Meditate on these words. As you prepare to enter into prayer and fasting, what are the rules of engagement you need to observe and follow? Before you pray, it is extremely important to take note of my words. "The words I am speaking to you are both spirit and life (John 6.63, NIV).

"Therefore, whoever hears these sayings of Mine and does them, I will liken him to a wise man who built his house on the rock; and the rain descended, the floods came, and the winds blew and beat on that house; and it did not fall, for it was founded on the rock. But everyone who hears these sayings of Mine and does not do them will be like a foolish man who built his house on the sand; and the rain descended, the floods came, and the winds blew and beat on that house; and it fell. And great was its fall" (Matt. 7.24-27). Pay careful attention to this teaching. It will change your prayer life and your life. Preparation and planning are crucial parts of fasting and praying.

Where Do I Start?

It is important to know where to start when you want to fast and pray. True prayer is prompted by the Holy Spirit. It must be ordered and directed by the Holy Spirit. Prayer must never be prompted by what you are going through. What you are going through should never order the direction of your prayer. Yet, this is often the case. Pressure prompts us to pray and often gives direction to our prayer. For example, if you are sick, you often find yourself praying for God to heal you. What if this is not the will of God? The Apostle Paul provides an example of a prayer he made based on his circumstances, as recorded in 2 Corinthians 12.7-9: "or because of these surpassingly great revelations. Therefore, in order to keep me from becoming conceited, I was given a thorn in my flesh, a messenger of Satan, to torment me. Three times I pleaded with the Lord to take it away from me. But he said to me, 'My grace is sufficient for you, for my power is made perfect in weakness.' Therefore I will boast all the more gladly about my weaknesses, so that Christ's power may rest on me."

The Apostle Paul wanted so much to be healed of his infirmity, which had been a significant challenge to him and his church. Under pressure, he prayed, but God rejected his plea. Through this, Apostle Paul learned that prayer must be prompted by the Holy Spirit. The Word of God bears witness to this: "The steps of a good man are ordered by the Lord" (Ps. 37.23).

Prayer that is prompted by our needs is often dangerous because it originates from the flesh. We cannot expect God to respond to the prompting of our flesh. God is Spirit, and those who worship Him must do so in spirit and truth. In John 6.63, it is written, "It is the Spirit who gives life; the flesh profits nothing." The Apostle Paul provides instructive teaching in Romans 8.6-11: "For to be carnally minded is death, but to be spiritually minded is life and peace. Because the carnal mind is enmity against God; for it is not subject to the law of God, nor indeed can be. So then, those who are in the flesh cannot please God. But you are not in the flesh but in the Spirit, if indeed the Spirit of God dwells in you. Now if anyone does not have the Spirit of Christ, he is not His. And if Christ is in you, the body is dead because of sin, but the Spirit is life because of righteousness."

Before you enter into prayer, ensure you have had enough time to meditate on the Word of God and prepare yourself spiritually.

How do you do this? Find time to read the Word of God. Read it slowly and reverentially. As you read, stop and ponder: Am I what the Word of God says? Where am I falling short? How can I align myself? Confront your weaknesses head-on. Examine yourself to see if you are still in the faith (2 Cor. 13.5). Many believers are afraid to search themselves. It is easy to search others, but can you search yourself honestly and truthfully? King David was an exceptionally wise and godly man. His candidness and brokenness in the face of his human frailty were remarkable. As a king with great power and authority, he understood that God expects integrity from everyone, whether king or servant. He expected us to search our inner man for any hidden faults or sins. In Psalms 19.12, David shows his sincerity in prayer: "Who can understand his errors? Cleanse me from secret faults." David knew that it is easy to see the sins of others but another level of spirituality to examine oneself and acknowledge, "Lord, I am wrong here." When you reach that level, you are on your way to defeating the devil. The devil often hides in our pride and unwillingness to search our hearts.

Get Rid of Sin

The Bible teaches us to, "Confess your trespasses to one another, and pray for one another, that you may be healed. The effective, fervent prayer of a righteous man avails much. Elijah was a man with a nature like ours, and he prayed earnestly that it would not rain; and it did not rain on the land for three years and six months. And he prayed again, and the heaven gave rain, and the earth produced its fruit" (Jas. 5.16-18). Sin is the greatest hindrance to prayer. It obstructs prayer. Where there is sin, God will not get involved unless you repent. In Isaiah 59.1-2, the prophet of God gives us a deep insight into what sin does to prayer: "Behold, the Lord's hand is not shortened, that it cannot save; nor His ear heavy, that it cannot hear. But your iniquities have separated you from your God; and your sins have hidden His face from you, so that He will not hear."

Sin damages our relationship with God and hinders our prayers. It is important to check where we have grieved the Holy Spirit before we try to seek or achieve dominion. Begin your journey on a clean slate, and you will be amazed by what you can accomplish.

A clean slate is only possible if we place our confidence in the finished work of the cross. Our righteousness is as "filthy rags" (Isa. 64.6). Christ died on the cross to remove the stench of sin and its poison and offer us His own righteousness. Through faith in Him, we may receive the righteousness of Christ. It's not what we can do to avoid sinning; despite our best efforts, we cannot overcome sin on our own.

Paul Describes this dilemma in Romans 7:14-25: "For we know that the law is spiritual, but I am carnal, sold under sin. For what I am doing, I do not understand. For what I will to do, that I do not practice; but what I hate, that I do. If, then, I do what I will not to do, I agree with the law that it is good. But now, it is no longer I who do it, but sin that dwells in me. For I know that in me (that is, in my flesh) nothing good dwells; for to will is present with me, but how to perform what is good I do not find. For the good that I will to do, I do not do; but the evil I will not to do, that I practice. Now if I do what I will not to do, it is no longer I who do it, but sin that dwells in me. I find then a law, that evil is present with me, the one who wills to do good. For I delight in the law of God according to the inward man. But I see another law in my members, warring against the law of my mind, and bringing me into captivity to the law of sin which is in my members. O wretched man that I am! Who will deliver me from this body of death? I thank God—through Jesus Christ our Lord!" (Rom. 7.14-25).

I will say it again, it's not what we can do on our own to avoid sinning; it is about what Jesus Christ accomplished on the cross to defeat sin and what He is doing in us to help us conquer the sinful nature. We are promised complete victory over sin by believing and acting on the finished work of atonement done on the cross of

Calvary. Be assured and guaranteed that you have power over sin and sin will not master you or have dominion over you. By dying on the cross of Calvary, Christ has offered you complete and total victory over sin. I can guarantee the refreshment that comes with faith in our incredible Saviour, Christ. By overcoming sin, you have given your life an opportunity to recalibrate and relaunch yourself for greatness.

This is your moment, the hour of your breakthrough. God has granted you a new lease on life. You can step out again in faith and take dominion over those things that were stumbling blocks to your success. Dominion and victory are intertwined; they are inseparable like Siamese twins. Gird the loins of your mind and stand in absolute faith in Christ—nothing but Christ is your security. Elevate your faith, seize opportunities and make the most of them. Be a careful planner and a consistent executor of ideas and revelations without succumbing to fear or doubt. There is no room for double-mindedness.

I am fully convinced that reading this book is not a mere act of chance but a God-given opportunity to rediscover yourself and realize your divine purpose. God meticulously planned your destiny and created a divine path for your life to follow. Here you are—reflect deeply. Summon your courage and faith, act on the word of God, and I see ahead of you an incredible, glorious, and unforgettable experience. Welcome to this new phase of your life, where dominion defines what you do and who you will become.

7

Achieving Dominion by Restoring Family Harmony

The family is the foundation and fabric of any given society or community. Broken families break things and lead to broken systems. It is at the family level where we must start. As the saying goes, "Charity begins at home." Yet, it is precisely at the family level where satan has focused his most severe attacks and opposition. He has made relentless efforts to undermine and sabotage families. We must address this issue right at the family level—no step higher or lower.

Many families are fragmented and polarized. Year after year, this vicious cycle of division continues to plague families. Christian homes have not been spared. Satan is relentlessly trying to tear families apart. But God has given us guidelines on how families ought to operate. God is a God of families: "A father of the fatherless, a defender of widows, is God in His holy habitation. God sets the solitary in families; He brings out those who are bound into prosperity; But the rebellious dwell in a dry land" (Psalms 68:5-6).

When God created Adam and Adam had the opportunity to name all the animals, there was something missing. This is an amazing story. Follow it through, and you will discover what I am saying. In

Genesis 2:18, it is written: "And the LORD God said, 'It is not good that man should be alone; I will make him a helper comparable to him.'"

God wanted Adam to have someone to fellowship with. God wanted to see a family. It was not just any kind of family; He wanted to see a blessed family. Someone might ask, how do we know this? We see it in God's promise to Adam and Eve's family in Genesis 1:27-29: "So God created man in His own image; in the image of God He created him; male and female He created them. Then God blessed them, and God said to them, 'Be fruitful and multiply; fill the earth and subdue it; have dominion over the fish of the sea, over the birds of the air, and over every living thing that moves on the earth.' And God said, 'See, I have given you every herb that yields seed which is on the face of all the earth, and every tree whose fruit yields seed; to you it shall be for food.'"

The family which God created was blessed and fruitful. This is the vision of God for the family, and it has never changed. God's plan unfolds for each generation. The Apostle Paul, writing to the Church in Ephesus, provided instructions on how families ought to follow God's vision: "Therefore be imitators of God as dear children. And walk in love, as Christ also has loved us and given Himself for us, an offering and a sacrifice to God for a sweet-smelling aroma" (Ephesians 5:1-2).

Submitting to one another in the fear of God. Wives, submit to your own husbands, as to the Lord. For the husband is head of the wife, as also Christ is head of the church; and He is the Savior of the body. Therefore, just as the church is subject to Christ, so let the wives be to their own husbands in everything. Husbands, love your wives, just as Christ also loved the church and gave Himself for her, that He might sanctify and cleanse her with the washing of water by the word, that He might present her to Himself a glorious church, not having spot or wrinkle or any such thing, but that she should be holy and without blemish. So husbands ought to love their own wives as their own bodies; he who loves his wife loves himself. For no one ever hated his own flesh, but nourishes and cherishes it, just as the Lord does the church. For we are members of His body, of His flesh and of His bones. 'For this reason a man shall leave his father and mother and be joined to his wife, and the two shall become one flesh.' This is a great mystery, but I speak concerning Christ and the church. Nevertheless, let each one of you in particular so love his own wife as himself, and let the wife see that she respects her husband. (Eph 5:21-33)

The picture Apostle Paul paints for the family is beautiful and profound. Yet, statistics show that in 2020 alone, 2.7 million people divorced in Canada. The rate of divorce and separation is increasing alarmingly each year. Most families have stopped using the Bible as the manual for their lives. Those who try to adhere to it often only pay lip service to the Word of God. Family members might live under the same roof, but they live separately. The wife may not know what the husband is doing, and the husband may not know what the wife is doing. As reflected in His Word, God's will is that the husband and wife should be one. Humanity has created its own trajectory: "Each man for himself, God for us all paradigm." Family cohesion and unity are no longer common values aspired to in the family. Husbands and wives hide things from each other. Married couples prefer to deal with outsiders rather than members of their family. Very few people see the family as the sacred and holy institution given to us by God to help us live the fullness of our lives. As a result, the blessing and potential of the family is lost. Children drift away from their parents; they do their own thing. This is the state year in and year out.

I want you to reflect on the state of your family. What are you doing to try to bring your family together? What have you done to contribute to the division and disintegration of your family? What steps are you taking to fix this state of affairs? When we live in a family that is torn apart, do we realize we are living in sin? When we cannot show affection to one another, we are in sin. Whether we like it or not, sin is destroying our lives. Psalms 133:1-3 is a powerful and moving song that contains profound advice to families that want to experience the blessing of God.

> Behold, how good and how pleasant it is for brethren to dwell together in unity! It is like the precious oil upon the head, running down on the beard, the beard of Aaron, running down on the edge of his garments. It is like the dew of Hermon, descending upon the mountains of Zion; For there the LORD commanded the blessing—Life forevermore. (Ps. 133:1-3)

The family that follows the precepts of God and His Word must be blessed. But in today's generation, very few families seriously seek to apply the Word to their family circumstances. Christians are living as if they are unbelievers. As you start your journey of achieving dominion, consider having a family meeting. Christian families need to come together and reorganize. Your family life must give glory to Christ. Communication is a crucial aspect of building the family. You cannot address the issues affecting your family unless you sit down as a family and discuss them. The best way to prepare for achieving dominion is for your family to reflect on what has been happening and map out a way forward together. The best is yet to come but remember, the best will only come to those who sit and plan for it. To keep a family together requires a carefully crafted, godly plan—one that must be respected and honoured. This plan requires implementation to remain effective and functional. Daily prayer and interaction are necessary to keep a family healthy and vibrant. I see God restoring the family back to its original place in theological history. I challenge this generation to be intentional where it concerns the family. The better the family cohesion, the better and more proper nation we can have.

8

Obtaining Dominion through Financial Stewardship

Organizing your personal finances is an indispensable step in preparing to achieve dominion. Money is crucial for day-to-day sustenance. We live in a world where nothing is free. We pay for everything we need. While we may access charitable food and clothing banks for free, someone somewhere is paying for those items. Nothing is truly free; this is the nature of the capitalist system in which we live. However, God has warned us in His Word: "For the love of money is a root of all kinds of evil, for which some have strayed from the faith in their greediness, and pierced themselves through with many sorrows" (1 Timothy 6:10).

In our quest to be debt-free and live a truly prosperous life without being ensnared by the devil, let us review the following scriptures to understand God's attitude towards money and stewardship:

- **1 Timothy 6:10:** "For the love of money is a root of all kinds of evil, for which some have strayed from the faith in their greediness, and pierced themselves through with many sorrows."
- **Matthew 6:24:** "No one can serve two masters; for either he will hate the one and love the other, or else he will be loyal to

the one and despise the other. You cannot serve God and mammon."
- **Hebrews 13:5:** "Let your conduct be without covetousness; be content with such things as you have. For He Himself has said, 'I will never leave you nor forsake you.'"
- **2 Timothy 3:2:** "For men will be lovers of themselves, lovers of money, boasters, proud, blasphemers, disobedient to parents, unthankful, unholy,"
- **1 Timothy 6:9-10:** "But those who desire to be rich fall into temptation and a snare, and into many foolish and harmful lusts which drown men in destruction and perdition."
- **Luke 12:15:** "And He said to them, 'Take heed and beware of covetousness, for one's life does not consist in the abundance of the things he possesses.'"

It is clear from these scriptures that God does not hate people having money; He owns the silver and gold. However, God desires that money have a proper place in our lives. Money must not rule us. The love of money is the root of all evil, and you cannot serve both God and money. Mishandling money can lead to disastrous consequences. I have seen many Christians who have destroyed their lives and integrity in pursuit of money, engaging in questionable conduct that undermines their Christian values.

I recall a time when I faced severe financial difficulty. I had no heating in my house during a harsh Canadian winter. With two small boys and mounting bills, I struggled even to afford bus fare of 49 cents. Despite my dire situation, a man offered me a large sum of money if I would halt church programs to shoot a movie and dress the church to resemble a Mormon church. I refused, maintaining my integrity despite the financial strain. Though some church members thought I was foolish, I knew I could not use scripture to justify something against God's will. A few weeks later, God provided a righteous solution to my financial problems. Remember, God is faithful.

God also wants us to be good stewards of what He provides. Are you a faithful steward? How do you manage your money? Many families lack the skills to manage their financial resources effectively. They do not budget or plan their spending. They shop impulsively without a list, failing to manage their finances. As you embark on your journey to achieving dominion, review your monthly budget. Consider how much money you need each month and for the whole year. Can you cover your expenses with your income?

Financial success results from God's blessing through good budgeting and stewardship. Commit to honouring God through diligent stewardship. Strive to eliminate debt and practice saving money. Avoid spending everything each month; every penny saved counts.

Dave Ramsey says, "A budget is telling your money where to go, instead of wondering where it went." Remember Jesus' teaching in Luke 16:10: "He who is faithful in what is least is faithful also in much; and he who is unjust in what is least is unjust also in much." No one can be blessed unless they learn to manage the little that God has given them. It will not be easy to overcome disorganization and poor spending habits, but make up your mind to change. Challenge yourself that you will not continue with the same habits that got you here in the first place. Give yourself a fresh start, as God has given you another opportunity.

9

Dominion through Embracing Your Divine Assignment

Good morning, believer. You've made it this far. You've taken the time to read through this book and have accumulated valuable insights and spiritual knowledge on preparing to achieve dominion. Now, it's time to step out confidently into the dominion that God has planned for you. You need to be motivated to start, believing that this is your divine assignment for the coming year. You cannot begin unless you truly BELIEVE in the purpose to which you are called.

Let us examine the life lessons of a few biblical figures. These individuals showed a remarkable understanding of their life assignments. Initially, their responses may have been wavering, unsure, or doubtful, but when they embraced their assignment, they would not let go. They refused to compromise; It was a matter of conviction. A man of great destiny is a man of conviction—one who stands firm in the face of opposition and hostility. It was their deep willingness to pay the price required to complete God's assignment for their lives. No one called by God can take their destiny lightly. Destinies are achieved by those willing to pay the extreme and costly price of achieving dominion. One must climb the ladder of life to reach the level of dominion before they can command the circumstances of their life to align with the will of God and achieve victory that will bring glory to Him.

There is no perfect place to start. There are no perfect circumstances to step out; only perfect faith to believe God for the completion of the assignment. One must be convinced that God, who gave the assignment, would supply the necessary tools to accomplish it. Conviction of faith is the perfect starting point. These great heroes of faith doubted but ultimately allowed God to speak. When the word of God came to their hearts, they had no option but to act in accordance with it. They knew in their inner being that when God says it, it is settled. Belief is our anchor and the basis of our connection.

Let us reflect on the lives of these biblical characters and be inspired to act on our conviction to achieve our life assignments.

Jeremiah Doubted His Assignment

The word of the Lord came to me, saying, 'Before I formed you in the womb I knew you; before you were born I sanctified you; I ordained you a prophet to the nations.' Then said I: 'Ah, Lord God! Behold, I cannot speak, for I am a youth.' But the Lord said to me: 'Do not say, "I am a youth," for you shall go to all to whom I send you, and whatever I command you, you shall speak. Do not be afraid of their faces, for I am with you to deliver you,' says the Lord. Then the Lord put forth His hand and touched my mouth, and the Lord said to me: 'Behold, I have put My words in your mouth. See, I have this day set you over the nations and over the kingdoms, to root out and to pull down, to destroy and to throw down, to build and to plant. (Jer. 1:4-10)

Isaiah Feared His Unworthiness

So I said: 'Woe is me, for I am undone! Because I am a man of unclean lips, and I dwell in the midst of a people of unclean lips; for my eyes have seen the King, the Lord of hosts.' Then one of the seraphim flew to me, having in his hand a live coal which he had taken with the tongs from the altar. And he touched my mouth with it, and said: 'Behold, this has touched your lips; your iniquity is taken away, and your sin purged.' Also I heard the voice of the Lord, saying: 'Whom shall I send, and who will go for Us?' Then I said, 'Here am I! Send me.'" (Isa. 6:5-8)

Moses Felt Inadequate

Then Moses answered and said, 'But suppose they will not believe me or listen to my voice; suppose they say, "The Lord has not appeared to you."' So the Lord said to him, 'What is that in your hand?' He said, 'A rod.' And He said, 'Cast it on the ground.' So he cast it on the ground, and it became a serpent; and Moses fled from it. Then the Lord said to Moses, 'Put your hand in your bosom.' And he put his hand in his bosom, and when he took it out, behold, his hand was leprous, like snow. And He said, 'Put your hand in your bosom again.' So he put his hand in his bosom again, and drew it out of his bosom, and behold, it was restored like his other flesh. Then it will be, if they do not believe you or heed the message of the first sign, that they may believe the message of the latter sign. And it shall be, if they do not believe even these two signs or listen to your voice, that you shall take water from the river and pour it on the dry land. The water which you take from the river will become blood on the dry land.' Then Moses said to the Lord, 'O my Lord, I am not eloquent, neither before nor since You have spoken to Your servant; but I am slow of speech and slow of tongue. (Exod. 4:1-10)

Gideon Questioned His Role

Now the Angel of the Lord came and sat under the terebinth tree which was in Ophrah, which belonged to Joash the Abiezrite, while his son Gideon threshed wheat in the winepress, in order to hide it from the Midianites. And the Angel of the Lord appeared to him, and said to him, 'The Lord is with you, you mighty man of valor!' Gideon said to Him, 'O my Lord, if the Lord is with us, why then has all this happened to us? And where are all His miracles which our fathers told us about, saying, "Did not the Lord bring us up from Egypt?" But now the Lord has forsaken us and delivered us into the hands of the Midianites. (Judg. 6:11-13)

Everyone who has been given an assignment by God has, at times, felt inadequate or ill-prepared, as these individuals did. You may also find your assignment overwhelming at times. Doubts may arise from within or from others. Nehemiah faced similar opposition from Sanballat and Tobiah; "But it so happened, when Sanballat heard that we were rebuilding the wall, that he was furious and very indignant, and mocked the Jews. And he spoke before his brethren and the army of Samaria, and said, "What are these feeble Jews doing? Will they fortify themselves? Will they offer sacrifices? Will they complete it in a day? Will they revive the stones from the heaps of rubbish—stones that are burned?" Now Tobiah the Ammonite was beside him, and he said, "Whatever they build, if even a fox goes up on it, he will break down their stone wall" (Nehemiah 4:1-3).

There is a secret to overcoming such doubts and opposition: trust God. Believe that you can do all things through Christ who strengthens you. God has an assignment for you as you start this journey of achieving dominion. Remember, you need Jesus Christ to accomplish it. In John 15:5, Jesus said: "I am the vine, you are the branches. He who abides in Me, and I in him, bears much fruit; for without Me you can do nothing."

God is faithful. Do not doubt. You cannot succeed in this new journey without faith. Believe in and act upon your beliefs. Achieving dominion is filled with promises and potential. You are destined for greatness. There is a comeback awaiting you. Step out in faith and make a difference. That first step matters. Do not hesitate or procrastinate. Many people have hesitated and procrastinated, and lost opportunities. Do not fall into the trap of "I am waiting for the perfect time." It's an illusion the devil offers to believers, suggesting there will be a perfect time. Many religious Christians say, "I am waiting for confirmation." Sometimes God never provides a second confirmation on a particular and specific assignment. Satan seduces us into thinking that a perfect time will come, allowing us to act on God's word for our lives. Do not be trapped by the devil's deceitfulness.

Consider biblical figures: When Jeremiah stepped out, he was a youth. when David fought Goliath, he had no military experience. When Joseph advised Potiphar, he was a prisoner. When Paul accepted his call, he was a murderer. Rahab saved the spies, while being a well-known prostitute. Ruth became the great-grandmother of our Lord Jesus when she was a Moabite. Mary Magdalene broke the jar of oil when she was known as a sinful woman in the city. Moses accepted the assignment to return to Egypt while being a fugitive from justice. Jacob became the Doyen of Israel's inheritance despite being known as a crook.

God specializes in taking imperfect people and turning them into mighty vessels for His use. He turns your mess into a message. Your weaknesses do not prevent Him from using you. As the Apostle Paul writes in 2 Corinthians 4.7, "But we have this treasure in earthen vessels, that the excellence of the power may be of God and not of us."

When reflecting on biblical characters, you will notice that God uses the foolish things of this world to confound the wise. This is because God's foolishness is wiser than the wisdom of men (1 Cor. 1.25). How can we see the power of God if we wait for a perfect time? When we believe God amidst imperfections and are willing to trust Him in the dark, that is the real evidence of faith. Faith demands evidence—evidence that you truly believe. David believed and trusted God, even though he has no military experience, to defeat the renowned Philistine army general. The simplicity of his faith, believing that a sling and five stones would win a huge battle, is the reflection of real faith. This is an example of the simplicity of conviction. Faith requires no complexity; it is a simple belief in God who is able and capable.

Your life must be simple yet accomplish mighty assignments for the Lord. The so-called imperfect time is the perfect time for anyone who believe in Jesus Christ. The abundance of one's weaknesses cannot stop the mighty strength of the Lord. Depend on God for the outcome of your life. Solomon wrote in Proverbs 3:5-6, "Trust in the

Lord with all your heart, and lean not on your own understanding; in all your ways acknowledge Him, and He shall direct your paths." All you need is to trust God, and in trusting God, the situation becomes perfect. It is God's presence in a situation that makes it the perfect time. It is God alone and absolutely God, that we must trust before we act.

www.ingramcontent.com/pod-product-compliance
Lightning Source LLC
Chambersburg PA
CBHW050445010526
44118CB00013B/1690